The 2012-2013 Baltimore Ravens:

The AFC Championship & the Road to the NFL 2013 Super Bowl

Dan Fathow

Megalodon Entertainment, LLC.

Published by Megalodon Entertainment, LLC. (USA)
www.MegalodonEntertainment.com

First Printing: January 2013

Copyright © 2013 Megalodon Entertainment LLC. All rights reserved.

All rights reserved under the International and Pan-American Copyright conventions. No part of this publication may be reproduced, or transmitted by any means in any form (electronic, photocopying, mechanical, recording, or any other method), without the specific written permission of the publisher. Please, direct questions to info@megalodonentertainment.com.

Printed in the United States of America.

ISBN: 978-1-61589-041-5
ISBN-10: 1-61589-041-6

The NFL, National Football League, Baltimore Ravens, Super Bowl, AFC, and all team names, locations, and events are ™ of their respective owners. No affiliation to any teams, players, or intellectual properties is claimed or implied by this publication.

BULK INQUERIES:
Quantity discounts are available on bulk orders of this novel for educational, fund-raising, promotional, and special sales purposes. For details, please contact www.MegalodonEntertainment.com

Check Out Another Great Book from Megalodon Entertainment LLC

From Lewis Aleman, Bestselling Author of Cold Streak & Faces in Time

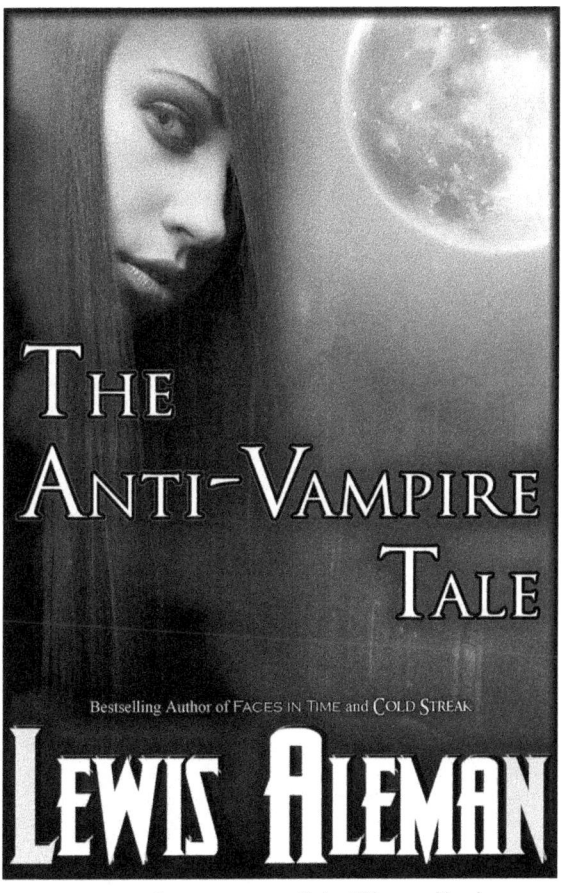

Simon is a vampire, prowling through the dark New Orleans streets that pulse with wild adventure and fangs gleaming in the shadows. He's spent the last few decades as a recluse, aching over a lost love. Now, he's put it behind him, thirsting to fulfill the raging inner need he's deprived himself for so long.

Ruby feels isolated and out of place--lonely, shy, but too strong-minded to go along with the crowd. All that changes when she is dragged out for her birthday and ends up dancing with Simon--mysterious, blue-eyed, and gorgeous. Her body tingles watching his muscled form move--so fast, so smooth, so powerful. His smile is otherworldly, and his kiss charges her with electric energy. All seems to be going well until three other vampires appear in the crowd, turning the dance floor into a horror show.

Real Vampires...Don't Sparkle

.com

Facebook.com/LewisAleman
Youtube.com/LewisAleman

Check Out More Great Releases from Megalodon Entertainment LLC

The Next Book in the Saga...

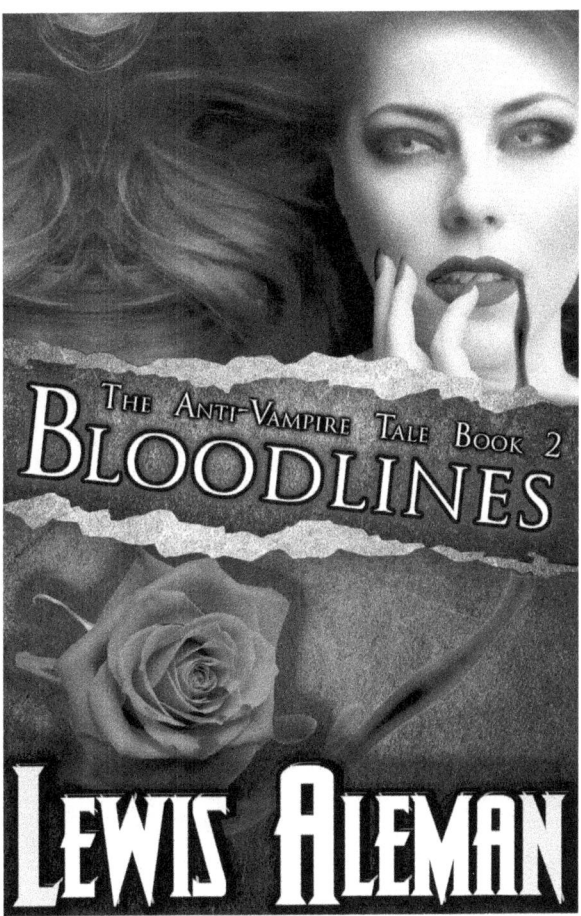

PRAISE FOR LEWIS ALEMAN:

"There is craftsmanship in Aleman's details; elaborate use of adjectival simile and metaphor ... stimulates ... memorable ... space-time research well done"
Dionne Charlet
Where Y'At Magazine
Feb 2010

"*Faces in Time* was an adventurous, fast paced, time traveling novel...loved the twists and turns...Lewis writes beautifully, his work is filled with great detailed descriptions...a great adventure. I haven't seen anything out like it."
La Femme Readers
December 12, 2009

ISBN-13: 978-1-61589-028-6
ISBN: 1-61589-028-9

WWW.LEWISALEMAN.COM
FACEBOOK.COM/LEWISALEMAN
YOUTUBE.COM/LEWISALEMAN

The 2012-2013 Baltimore Ravens:

The AFC Championship & the Road to the NFL 2013 Superbowl

Dan Fathow

Megalodon Entertainment, LLC.

Table of Contents

Part I: 2012 AFC Championship Season

Week 1   vs. Cincinnati Bengals 13

Week 2   vs. Philadelphia Eagles 17

Week 3   vs. New England Patriots 21

Week 4   vs. Cleveland Browns 25

Week 5   vs. Kansas City Chiefs 29

Week 6   vs. Dallas Cowboys 33

Week 7   vs. Houston Texans 37

Week 8 (Bye Week – no content)

Week 9   vs. Cleveland Browns 41

Week 10 vs. Oakland Raiders 45

Week 11 vs. Pittsburgh Steelers 49

Week 12 vs. San Diego Chargers 53

Week 13 vs. Pittsburgh Steelers 57

Week 14 vs. Washington Redskins 63

Week 15 vs. Denver Broncos 67

Week 16 vs. New York Giants 71

Week 17 vs. Cincinnati Bengals 77

Week 18 vs. Indianapolis Colts 81

Week 19 vs. Denver Broncos 85

Week 20 vs. New England Patriots 89

PART II: **SUPER BOWL XLVII
   THE MATCHUP VS. THE 49ERS 97**

PART III: **THE QUARTERBACK MATCHUP
   FLACCO VS KAEPERNICK 100**

Part I:
The Magnificent Season

WEEK 1

September 10, 2012
M&T Bank Stadium – Baltimore, MD

Teams	1st	2nd	3rd	4th	Total
Cincinnati Bengals	0	10	3	0	**13**
Baltimore Ravens	10	7	17	10	**44**

GAME SUMMARY

The opening game of the Ravens' 2012 season pitted them against the Cincinnati Bengals at home. While the Ravens were the heavy favorites in this game, fans and the sports world watched with great interest to see how the Ravens would look, having seen them last lose to the New England Patriots in the previous season's AFC Championship Game.

With a regular season record of 12-4 and a post-season record of 1-1 in 2011, expectations were high for the Ravens in 2012. Fans were hoping for another spectacular year, hopefully ending in a Super Bowl appearance, and critics were looking for signs that the Ravens might not have what it would take to beat a high caliber team like the Patriots in the post-season.

With a 44-13 trouncing of the Bengals, the Ravens made a powerful statement, showing that they were a championship team, deserving of notice.

In the game, Joe Flacco put up impressive numbers. The quarterback threw for 299 yards on 21 of 29 passes, with 2 touchdowns and 0 interceptions.

Scoring 2 rushing and 2 passing touchdowns, the Ravens were excelling in the air and on the ground. With 308 passing yards to 122 rushing, the offense was a little more successful passing than running.

Baltimore also won the turnover war, 2-0. Total yards also clearly went to the Ravens 430 yards to 322 yards. When a team puts up over 100 more offensive yards and wins the turnover battle, they typically win, and win big, as is what happened in this game.

TEAM LEADERS

Passing

Joe Flacco #5
299 Yards, 2 Touchdowns, 0 Interceptions
(21/29, 72.41 Comp %)

Rushing

Ray Rice #27
68 Yards on 10 Carries
6.8 Yards per Carry
2 Rushing Touchdowns

Bernard Pierce #30
19 Yards on 4 Carries
4.75 Yards per Carry
0 Rushing Touchdowns

2012 – 2013 Baltimore Ravens 15

Anthony Allen #35
13 Yards on 4 Carries
3.25 Yards per Carry
0 Rushing Touchdowns

Receiving

Dennis Pitta #88
73 Yards on 5 Receptions
14.6 Yards per Reception
1 Touchdown Reception

Anquan Boldin #81
63 Yards on 4 Receptions
15.75 Yards per Reception
1 Touchdown Reception

Torrey Smith #82
57 Yards on 2 Receptions
28.5 Yards per Reception
0 Touchdown Receptions

Jacoby Jones #12
46 Yards on 3 Receptions
15.33 Yards per Reception
0 Touchdown Receptions

Kicking

Justin Tucker #9
14 Points Total
3/3 Field Goals
5/5 Extra Points

Dan Fathow 16

Interceptions

Ed Reed #20
1 Interception

The Bottom Line

1 - 0

WEEK 2

September 16, 2012
Lincoln Financial Field – Philadelphia, PA

Teams	1st	2nd	3rd	4th	Total
Philadelphia Eagles	7	0	10	7	**24**
Baltimore Ravens	7	10	0	6	**23**

GAME SUMMARY

After routing the Cincinnati Bengals in Week 1, the Ravens were expected to beat the Eagles in Week 2. It's important to note and hard to remember that the Philadelphia Eagles were 1-0, coming into Week 2.

By season's end, the Eagles would accumulate the unimpressive record of 4-12, winning only 2 more games all season long after this contest. With that in mind, it's easy to discredit the Eagles as poor competition, but they did do some things right in this game.

The Eagles managed to out-rush and out-pass the Ravens in this contest, the bigger difference being 357 passing yards to Baltimore's 214. Philadelphia was also 1 for 1 on 4th down, while the Ravens were 0 for 2. 3rd-down efficiency was not much better as the Eagles were 7 for 15 and the Ravens were 4 for 14. When your competition converts nearly twice as much as you on 3rd down, it's going to be a rough day.

Although Michael Vick and the Eagles struggled nearly the entire season, unfortunately for the Ravens, this was by far

Vick's best performance of the year. He threw for 371 yards (a season high), 1 touchdown, and 2 interceptions. This game also marked Vick's only rushing touchdown of 2012, without which his team may have not been victorious.

The biggest surprise of the day is that the Eagles managed to win while losing the turnover battle, 4-2.

Joe Flacco threw for 232 yards on 22 of 42 passes for 1 touchdown and 1 interception. Barring the interception, it was not a bad statistical day for the quarterback.

Running back Ray Rice probably had the best outing for the team, rushing for 99 yards. Sadly, the next highest rusher was Vonta Leach with 5 yards. Rice accounted for 89.2% of all of Baltimore's rushing yards in this game. Top that off with Rice's 53 receiving yards, and it was a great day for him, despite the loss.

Another very notable performance was in Ed Reed nabbing his second interception in 2 games.

TEAM LEADERS

Passing

Joe Flacco #5
232 Yards, 1 Touchdown, 1 Interception
(22/42, 52.38 Comp %)

Rushing

Ray Rice #27
99 Yards on 16 Carries
6.18 Yards per Carry
0 Rushing Touchdowns

2012 – 2013 Baltimore Ravens 19

Vonta Leach #44
5 Yards on 1 Carry
5.00 Yards per Carry
1 Rushing Touchdown

Receiving

Dennis Pitta #88
65 Yards on 8 Receptions
8.13 Yards per Reception
0 Touchdown Receptions

Ray Rice #27
53 Yards on 6 Receptions
8.83 Yards per Reception
0 Touchdown Reception

Torrey Smith #82
51 Yards on 2 Receptions
25.5 Yards per Reception
0 Touchdown Receptions

Jacoby Jones #12
21 Yards on 1 Reception
21 Yards per Reception
1 Touchdown Reception

Kicking

Justin Tucker #9
11 Points Total
3/3 Field Goals
2/2 Extra Points

DAN FATHOW 20

Interceptions

Ed Reed #20
1 Interception

Bernard Pollard #31
1 Interception

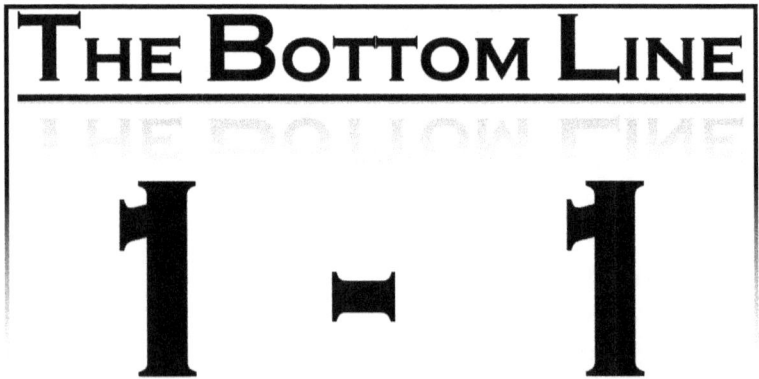

2012 – 2013 BALTIMORE RAVENS 21

WEEK 3

September 23, 2012
M&T Bank Stadium – Baltimore, MD

Teams	1st	2nd	3rd	4th	**Total**
New England Patriots	13	7	7	3	**30**
Baltimore Ravens	0	14	7	10	**31**

GAME SUMMARY

Even though both teams entered this contest with a 1-1 record, few picked the Ravens to beat the Patriots. This was certainly a grudge match as the Patriots crushed the Ravens' playoff hopes the last time they met in the AFC Championship game on January 22, 2012.

The big news of the game, unfortunately, was very sad news that was much bigger and more important than even 2 titanic rival teams meeting.

Wide receiver Torrey Smith's younger brother, Tevin, died in a motorcycle accident less than 24 hours before the game. According to Smith, he had less than an hour's sleep the night before the game, and he was uncertain if he would play for most of the day.

Smith not only decided to play in the game but was the team's leading receiver with 127 yards and 2 touchdowns. Without Smith's brave contributions in the face of personal tragedy, it is unlikely that the Ravens would have pulled off their narrow 1-point victory over the Patriots.

Rising to the challenge of facing one of the game's premier quarterbacks in Tom Brady, Flacco had a great game, throwing for 382 yards, 3 touchdowns, and 1 interception, besting Brady who also had a great game, but put up smaller numbers of 335 yards and 1 touchdown.

While the Ravens lost the turnover war 1-0 and giving up more penalty yards (135 yards to 10 yards), they certainly won total offensive yards 503 yards to 396 yards.

It's important to point out that kicker Jacoby Jones was perfect at this point in the season, accounting for 32 points on 7/7 field goals and 11/11 extra points.

This game was a huge win for the Ravens, bouncing back from the previous week's road loss, and proving that they can beat anyone in the NFL. They also dealt rival New England Patriots a hefty loss, dropping them to a 1-2 losing record, something no experts had predicted for the Patriots.

TEAM LEADERS

Passing

Joe Flacco #5
382 Yards, 3 Touchdowns, 1 Interception
(28/39, 71.79 Comp %)

Rushing

Ray Rice #27
101 Yards on 20 Carries
5.05 Yards per Carry
1 Rushing Touchdown

2012 – 2013 Baltimore Ravens 23

Bernard Pierce #30
17 Yards on 4 Carry
4.25 Yards per Carry
0 Rushing Touchdowns

Receiving

Torrey Smith #82
127 Yards on 6 Receptions
21.17 Yards per Reception
2 Touchdown Receptions

Jacoby Jones #12
86 Yards on 3 Receptions
28.67 Yards per Reception
0 Touchdown Receptions

Dennis Pitta #88
50 Yards on 5 Receptions
10 Yards per Reception
1 Touchdown Reception

Ray Rice #27
49 Yards on 5 Receptions
9.8 Yards per Reception
0 Touchdown Receptions

Anquan Boldin #81
48 Yards on 4 Receptions
12.00 Yards per Reception
0 Touchdown Receptions

Kicking

Dan Fathow 24

Justin Tucker #9
7 Points Total
1/1 Field Goals
4/4 Extra Points

Interceptions

None

WEEK 4

September 27, 2012
M&T Bank Stadium – Baltimore, MD

Teams	1st	2nd	3rd	4th	Total
Cleveland Browns	0	0	0	6	**6**
Baltimore Ravens	0	10	0	3	**13**

GAME SUMMARY

So the 0-3, Cleveland Browns were not supposed to be the best competition for the Baltimore Ravens coming off a victory over the New England Patriots, but it ended being a reasonably close contest.

The Browns lost in rushing yards (43-101), receiving yards (314-337), and turnovers (2-1). So, how did they keep this to a one-score game? The Browns did have penalty yards in their favor, giving up only 66 yards to the Ravens' 100 yards.

The other strong point of the Browns was that they had 4 sacks for a loss of 19 yards, where the Ravens only sacked the Browns once for a loss of 6 yards. Sacks are also a deceptive statistic in that their effect goes much further than the yardage loss in that it breaks momentum and rattles the quarterback.

Joe Flacco had a great game throwing for 356 yards (the second week in a row that he threw for over 350 yards), 1 touchdown, 1 interception, and a 60.87 completion percentage. Besides his passing accomplishments, Flacco also ran in a touchdown of his own.

Dan Fathow 26

Team Leaders

Passing

Joe Flacco #5
356 Yards, 1 Touchdown, 1 Interception
(28/46, 60.87 Comp %)

Rushing

Ray Rice #27
49 Yards on 18 Carries
2.72 Yards per Carry
0 Rushing Touchdowns

Bernard Pierce #30
48 Yards on 6 Carries
8.00 Yards per Carry
0 Rushing Touchdowns

Joe Flacco #5
4 Yards on 2 Carries
2.00 Yards per Carry
1 Rushing Touchdown

2012 – 2013 Baltimore Ravens 27

Receiving

Anquan Boldin #81
131 Yards on 9 Receptions
14.56 Yards per Reception
0 Touchdown Receptions

Torrey Smith #82
97 Yards on 6 Receptions
16.17 Yards per Reception
1 Touchdown Reception

Ray Rice #27
47 Yards on 8 Receptions
5.88 Yards per Reception
0 Touchdown Receptions

Kicking

Justin Tucker #9
5 Points Total
1/2 Field Goals
2/2 Extra Points

Interceptions

Cary Williams #29
1 Interception
Ran Back for a Touchdown

DAN FATHOW 28

THE BOTTOM LINE

3 - 1

WEEK 5

October 7, 2012
Arrowhead Stadium – Kansas City, MO

Teams	1st	2nd	3rd	4th	Total
Kansas City Chiefs	0	3	0	3	6
Baltimore Ravens	3	0	6	0	9

GAME SUMMARY

The Kansas City Chiefs were 1-3 coming into the game to meet the 3-1 Baltimore Ravens. What ensued was a low-scoring defensive war, with the Ravens coming out on top by 3 points.

All points in this game were scored by both teams' kickers. While Justin Tucker missed his first field goal of the season in the previous week's game, he certainly returned to form in this encounter, going 3 for 3.

The Chiefs won the turnover battle 4-2.

On the offensive front, the Ravens had the most passing yards, 165 to 124, while the Chiefs won the ground battle, rushing for 214 yards to Baltimore's 133. Kansas City had 3 more penalties for 27 more yards.

Joe Flacco had an off-day, only passing for 187 yards (slightly less than half the yards he put up against the Patriots) with 0 touchdowns and 1 interception.

Ray Rice had another impressive day, receiving for 102 yards on 17 grabs.

On the rushing front, Anquan Boldin was the clear leader, putting 82 yards under his feet on 4 carries.

Team Leaders

Passing

Joe Flacco #5
187 Yards, 0 Touchdowns, 1 Interception
(13/27, 48.15 Comp %)

Rushing

Ray Rice #27
102 Yards on 17 Carries
6.00 Yards per Carry
0 Rushing Touchdowns

Joe Flacco #5
14 Yards on 3 Carries
4.67 Yards per Carry
0 Rushing Touchdowns

Receiving

Anquan Boldin #81
82 Yards on 4 Receptions
20.5 Yards per Reception
0 Touchdown Receptions

2012 – 2013 Baltimore Ravens 31

Torrey Smith #82
38 Yards on 3 Receptions
12.67 Yards per Reception
0 Touchdown Receptions

Kicking

Justin Tucker #9
9 Points Total
3/3 Field Goals
0/0 Extra Points

Interceptions

Cary Williams #29
1 Interception

Lardarius Webb #21
1 Interception

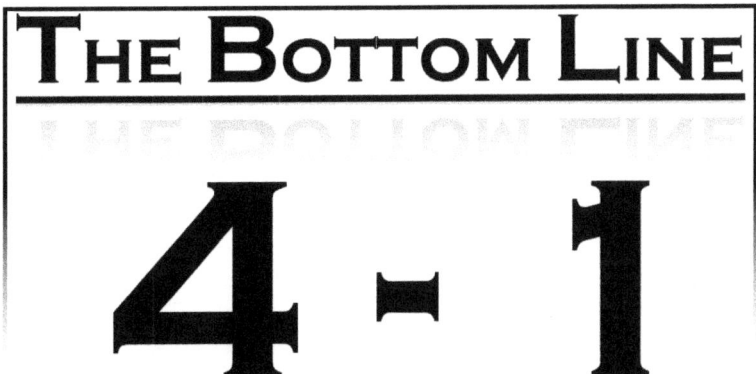

The Bottom Line

4 - 1

2012 – 2013 Baltimore Ravens 33

WEEK 6

October 14, 2012
M&T Bank Stadium – Baltimore, MD

Teams	1st	2nd	3rd	4th	Total
Dallas Cowboy	7	3	10	9	29
Baltimore Ravens	3	14	7	7	31

GAME SUMMARY

After the previous week's low-scoring defensive battle, the Ravens' 31-29 defeat of the Dallas Cowboys, provided a lot more offensive pyrotechnics.

Coming into this game, the Cowboys were 2-2 and looking to embark on a winning record. At 4-1, the Ravens already had their eyes on securing a playoff berth, and getting a victory over the dangerous but inconsistent Dallas Cowboys was the next step on their journey.

Baltimore won the turnover battle, 1-0, and they came out slightly ahead on penalties, committing 3 less than their opponents accounting for 6 fewer yards.

Despite coming up short on total yards, rushing yards, and passing yards, the Ravens managed to make the right plays at the right time to win this game.

Joe Flacco did not put up his highest numbers in this game, but he did have a 65.38 completion percentage on 234 yards, 1 touchdown, and 0 interceptions. That is a solid and consistent performance.

It was another great day for Anquan Boldin who caught for 98 yards. The next highest receiver was Ray Rice with 43 yards, who also rushed for 63 yards and 2 touchdowns. The 2 of them combined for a total of 204 offensive yards. Being that the Ravens team total was 316 yards, these two athletes accounted for 65% of Baltimore's offensive gains.

Justin Tucker was flawless, accounting for 7 points on a 38-yard field goal and 4 extra points.

One of the telling stats in this game was that the Dallas Cowboys had possession of the ball for 40:03, while the Ravens had possession for half of that at 19:57. Obviously the Ravens made their time with the ball count for much more, as they edged the Cowboys by 2 points.

Team Leaders

Passing

Joe Flacco #5
234 Yards, 1 Touchdown, 0 Interceptions
(17/26, 65.38 Comp %)

Rushing

Ray Rice #27
33 Yards on 16 Carries
2.06 Yards per Carry
2 Rushing Touchdowns

Bernard Pierce #30
21 Yards on 4 Carries
5.25 Yards per Carry
0 Rushing Touchdowns

2012 – 2013 Baltimore Ravens 35

Receiving

Anquan Boldin #81
98 Yards on 5 Receptions
19.6 Yards per Reception
0 Touchdown Receptions

Ray Rice #27
43 Yards on 1 Reception
43.00 Yards per Reception
0 Touchdown Receptions

Dennis Pitta #88
33 Yards on 4 Receptions
8.25 Yards per Reception
0 Touchdown Receptions

Torrey Smith #82
24 Yards on 2 Receptions
12.00 Yards per Reception
1 Touchdown Reception

Kicking

Justin Tucker #9
7 Points Total
1/1 Field Goals
4/4 Extra Points

Dan Fathow 36

Interceptions

Cary Williams #29
1 Interception

The Bottom Line

5 - 1

2012 – 2013 BALTIMORE RAVENS 37

WEEK 7

October 21, 2012
Reliant Stadium – Houston, TX

Teams	1st	2nd	3rd	4th	Total
Houston Texans	9	20	7	7	43
Baltimore Ravens	3	0	7	3	13

GAME SUMMARY

Week 7 caught the eye of the sports world as the 5-1 Ravens met the 5-1 Houston Texans. Both teams were being picked to make the playoffs, being 2 of the premier teams in the NFL, and football fans everywhere were eager to see them fight it out.

Before this contest, the Ravens had beaten the Texans in all 6 of their previous matchups, including bumping the Texans out of the playoffs in 2011.

This road game to Houston proved to be a difficult one for the Ravens to get their bearings. This far into the season, the only team to have gotten the better of the Texans was a desperate Green Bay team in week 6. There was no doubt about it, that the Texans were a hot team, destined for the playoffs, and they were stiff competition for any opponent. The Ravens would certainly have the last laugh in the 2012-2013 season by making it all the way to the Super Bowl and by beating the Patriots who ousted the Texans from the playoffs.

However, in this game, Baltimore was on the short end of the stick on turnovers (2-0), rushing yards (held to only 55 yards), passing yards (121-239). The total yardage was not pretty with Houston earning 420 yards to the Ravens' 176 yards.

Joe Flacco did not have a great game at all, completing 21 of 43 passes for 147 yards with 1 touchdown and 2 interceptions. His 48.83 completion percentage reflects his team's overall performance. He was also sacked 4 times, twice as much as his counterpart Matt Schaub was sacked.

Ray Rice was nearly all of the rushing offense for the Ravens, running for 42 yards on 9 carries. The next leading rusher was quarterback Joe Flacco, who only accounted for 7 yards.

Kicker Justin Tucker was flawless, putting the ball through the uprights on 2 of 2 field goals and 1 of 1 extra points.

Team Leaders

Passing

Joe Flacco #5
147 Yards, 1 Touchdown, 2 Interceptions
(21/43, 48.83 Comp %)

Rushing

Ray Rice #27
42 Yards on 9 Carries
4.67 Yards per Carry
0 Rushing Touchdown

2012 – 2013 Baltimore Ravens 39

Receiving

Torrey Smith #82
41 Yards on 4 Receptions
12.00 Yards per Reception
0 Touchdown Receptions

Dennis Pitta #88
33 Yards on 5 Receptions
6.60 Yards per Reception
0 Touchdown Receptions

Anquan Boldin #81
24 Yards on 3 Receptions
8.0 Yards per Reception
0 Touchdown Receptions

Tandon Doss #17
15 Yards on 1 Reception
15.00 Yards per Reception
1 Touchdown Reception

Kicking

Justin Tucker #9
7 Points Total
2/2 Field Goals
1/1 Extra Points

DAN FATHOW 40

Interceptions

none

THE BOTTOM LINE

5 - 2

2012 – 2013 BALTIMORE RAVENS 41

WEEK 9

November 4, 2012
Cleveland Browns Stadium – Cleveland, OH

Teams	1st	2nd	3rd	4th	Total
Cleveland Browns	0	9	3	3	**15**
Baltimore Ravens	14	0	0	11	**25**

GAME SUMMARY

Coming off a week 8 bye week, the Ravens were on the road and faced a 2-6 Cleveland Browns team. The 10-point victory is about what one would expect in this matchup, and it's exactly what the Ravens needed to right their ship to the playoffs following their loss to the Texans.

The ground game was close but won by the Ravens 137 yards to 116. The air battle was another close one, but the Browns barely edged out the Ravens 174 to 145 yards.

One of the big differences in this game was the turnover battle. The Ravens did not give up the ball, but Browns quarterback Brandon Weeden threw 2 interceptions.

Joe Flacco had another mediocre but steady game as he threw for 153 yards on 15 of 24 passes for 1 touchdown with 0 interceptions.

Becoming as consistent as death and taxes, Ray Rice rushed for 98 yards on 25 carries and 1 touchdown. Torrey

Smith also caught a touchdown pass, showing that the Ravens were deadly in the air and on the ground.

Team Leaders

Passing

Joe Flacco #5
153 Yards, 1 Touchdown, 0 Interceptions
(15/24, 62.50 Comp %)

Rushing

Ray Rice #27
98 Yards on 25 Carries
3.92 Yards per Carry
1 Rushing Touchdown

Bernard Pierce #30
26 Yards on 7 Carries
3.71 Yards per Carry
1 Rushing Touchdown

Receiving

Anquan Boldin #81
57 Yards on 5 Receptions
11.40 Yards per Reception
0 Touchdown Receptions

2012 – 2013 Baltimore Ravens 43

Torrey Smith #82
46 Yards on 4 Receptions
11.50 Yards per Reception
1 Touchdown Reception

Dennis Pitta #88
33 Yards on 2 Receptions
16.20 Yards per Reception
0 Touchdown Receptions

Kicking

Justin Tucker #9
5 Points Total
1/1 Field Goals
2/2 Extra Points

Interceptions

Cary Williams #29
1 Interception

Ed Reed #20
1 Interception

Dan Fathow 44

The Bottom Line

6 - 2

WEEK 10

November 11, 2012
M&T Bank Stadium – Baltimore, MD

Teams	1st	2nd	3rd	4th	Total
Oakland Raiders	0	10	7	3	**20**
Baltimore Ravens	10	17	21	7	**55**

GAME SUMMARY

The 2-6 Oakland Raiders were no match for the Ravens, who obliterated them by 35 points. This home game blowout showcased all of the Ravens' weapons, proving that they were a Super Bowl contender.

While the Oakland Raiders barely won total points by 3 yards, they lost the turnover battle 3-1, which is a recipe for losing games in the NFL.

Joe Flacco returned to top form and had a fantastic game, passing for 341 yards on 21 of 33 attempts for 3 touchdowns and 1 interception. Flacco's counterpart, Carson Palmer also had a great day throwing for 368 yards but 1 less touchdown and 1 interception. Between the 2 gun-slinging quarterbacks, it was quite an explosive game for fans to watch.

Both teams had similar passing and rushing yards, but once again, the Ravens capitalized much more on their opportunities, scoring a staggering 35 more points than their opponent.

It was not the best rushing day for either team. Ray Rice who had been on fire was held to just 35 yards, but he couldn't be kept out of the end zone as he scored a rushing touchdown.

The passing game was much more efficient with 4 players receiving for over 50 yards a piece. Dennis Pitta and Torrey Smith were the leaders, both catching passes for 67 yards each. Smith had 2 touchdown grabs, and Pitta had 1 of his own.

Once again, Justin Tucker was perfect nailing 2 of 2 field goals and 7 of 7 extra points, accounting for 13 points.

Team Leaders

Passing

Joe Flacco #5
341 Yards, 3 Touchdowns, 1 Interception
(21/33, 63.64 Comp %)

Rushing

Ray Rice #27
35 Yards on 13 Carries
2.69 Yards per Carry
1 Rushing Touchdown

Bernard Pierce #30
23 Yards on 10 Carries
2.30 Yards per Carry
0 Rushing Touchdowns

2012 – 2013 Baltimore Ravens 47

Sam Koch #4
7 Yards on 1 Carries
7.00 Yards per Carry
1 Rushing Touchdown

Receiving

Dennis Pitta #88
67 Yards on 5 Receptions
13.40 Yards per Reception
1 Touchdown Reception

Torrey Smith #82
67 Yards on 3 Receptions
33.50 Yards per Reception
2 Touchdown Receptions

Ed Dickson #84
59 Yards on 2 Receptions
29.50 Yards per Reception
0 Touchdown Receptions

Jacoby Jones #12
54 Yards on 2 Receptions
27.00 Yards per Reception
0 Touchdown Receptions

Anquan Boldin #81
38 Yards on 4 Receptions
9.50 Yards per Reception
0 Touchdown Receptions

Dan Fathow 48

Kicking

Justin Tucker #9
13 Points Total
2/2 Field Goals
7/7 Extra Points

Interceptions

Paul Kruger #99
1 Interception

The Bottom Line

7 - 2

2012 – 2013 Baltimore Ravens 49

Week 11

November 18, 2012
Heinz Field – Pittsburgh, PA

Teams	1st	2nd	3rd	4th	Total
Pittsburgh Steelers	7	0	3	0	**10**
Baltimore Ravens	10	0	3	0	**13**

GAME SUMMARY

The matchup between the 7-2 Ravens and the 6-3 Pittsburgh Steelers was one that both teams' fans were watching with anticipation and anxiety. Both teams posed a serious threat, and it was going to be a tough battle for everyone involved.

Baltimore gave up more penalty yards, had less rushing yards, and had less passing yards. In addition to that, the Ravens had the ball for about 6 minutes less than the Steelers.

So, how on earth did they win?

Ball control was the key factor in this game. Pittsburgh had 3 turnovers (2 fumbles and 1 interception), and the Ravens were perfect with 0 turnovers. In addition to that, as in some past games, the Ravens seemed to find a way to capitalize more on the scoreboard with less time and less yardage than their opponents.

Joe Flacco did not put up big yards, only throwing for 164 yards on 20 of 32 passing attempts, throwing for less than half the yards as he did the week before, but once again, he did not throw a single interception, which was crucial in this game.

More than half of the Ravens' points came from the sure foot of Justin Tucker, nailing 2 of 3 field goals and 1 extra point.

Team Leaders

Passing

Joe Flacco #5
164 Yards, 3 Touchdowns, 1 Interception
(20/32, 63.64 Comp %)

Rushing

Ray Rice #27
40 Yards on 20 Carries
2.00 Yards per Carry
0 Rushing Touchdowns

Bernard Pierce #30
8 Yards on 2 Carries
4.00 Yards per Carry
0 Rushing Touchdowns

2012 – 2013 Baltimore Ravens 51

Receiving

Anquan Boldin #81
79 Yards on 8 Receptions
9.88 Yards per Reception
0 Touchdown Receptions

Ray Rice #27
53 Yards on 5 Receptions
10.6 Yards per Reception
0 Touchdown Receptions

Bernard Pierce #30
11 Yards on 1 Reception
11.00 Yards per Reception
0 Touchdown Receptions

Ed Dickson #84
8 Yards on 2 Receptions
4.00 Yards per Reception
0 Touchdown Receptions

Kicking

Justin Tucker #9
7 Points Total
2/3 Field Goals
1/1 Extra Points

DAN FATHOW 52

Interceptions

Corey Graham #24
1 Interception

THE BOTTOM LINE

8 - 2

Week 12

November 25, 2012
Qualcomm Stadium – San Diego, CA

Teams	1st	2nd	3rd	4th	OT	Total
San Diego Chargers	0	10	0	3	0	**13**
Baltimore Ravens	0	0	3	10	3	**16**

GAME SUMMARY

A 0-10 halftime score, with the 8-2 Ravens trailing the 4-6 Chargers was very unexpected. The Ravens wouldn't get on the scoreboard until the 3rd quarter, but even then it would only be with a 3-point field goal.

However, the 4th quarter belonged to Baltimore as they put up 10 points while keeping the Chargers to only 3 more points, resulting in a tie 13-13 score, sending the game into overtime.

The Ravens delivered under pressure in overtime setting up kicker Justin Tucker for the game-winning field goal, propelling their team to a 9-2 record and sending the Chargers dropping down to 4-7.

Ball control was excellent for both teams; neither one surrendered a single turnover.

The Ravens were dominant in total yards with 443 to 280 yards: 316 to 189 passing yards and 127 to 91 rushing yards.

One of the key stats in this game was 3rd down efficiency. The Ravens went 12 for 24 on third down, while the Chargers only went 3 for 15. Baltimore racked up 25 first downs while San Diego only moved the chains 16 times.

Joe Flacco had an amazing game, throwing for 355 yards on 30 of 51 attempts with 1 touchdown and 0 interceptions. In this game as in past games, Flacco's low interception statistics were key in the Ravens' victory.

Besides Flacco, the two most dominant players on offense were Torrey Smith and Ray Rice. Smith caught 7 passes for a total of 144 yards. Rice rushed for 97 yards and received for another 67 yards. The 2 of them were responsible for a combined 308 yards, which was 70% of the Ravens' total offense in this encounter.

Justin Tucker was once again perfect in this outing, nailing 3 of 3 field goals and 1 extra point.

TEAM LEADERS

Passing

Joe Flacco #5
355 Yards, 1 Touchdown, 0 Interceptions
(30/51, 58.82 Comp %)

Rushing

Ray Rice #27
97 Yards on 22 Carries
4.41 Yards per Carry
0 Rushing Touchdowns

2012 – 2013 Baltimore Ravens 55

Bernard Pierce #30
34 Yards on 9 Carries
3.78 Yards per Carry
0 Rushing Touchdowns

Receiving

Torrey Smith #82
144 Yards on 7 Receptions
20.57 Yards per Reception
0 Touchdown Receptions

Ray Rice #27
67 Yards on 8 Receptions
8.38 Yards per Reception
0 Touchdown Receptions

Jacoby Jones #12
50 Yards on 5 Receptions
10.00 Yards per Reception
0 Touchdown Receptions

Dennis Pitta #88
42 Yards on 6 Receptions
7.00 Yards per Reception
1 Touchdown Reception

Anquan Boldin #81
42 Yards on 2 Receptions
21.00 Yards per Reception
0 Touchdown Receptions

Dan Fathow 56

Kicking

Justin Tucker #9
10 Points Total
3/3 Field Goals
1/1 Extra Points

Interceptions

none

The Bottom Line

9 - 2

WEEK 13

December 2, 2012
M&T Bank Stadium – Baltimore, MD

Teams	1st	2nd	3rd	4th	Total
Pittsburgh Steelers	3	3	7	10	**23**
Baltimore Ravens	0	13	7	0	**20**

GAME SUMMARY

This game was a rematch of the game they played just 2 weeks before, in which the Ravens were victorious. At this point, the Steelers found themselves with a 6-5 record, still fighting for their chance at the playoffs. The 9-2 Ravens were in a much better position for the offseason. For the Steelers, winning this game was more important. The Steelers did not have the luxury of losing and still making the playoffs. The Ravens impressive record easily allowed for losing a game and still having a spot in the post season.

One of variables in this matchup was that starting quarterback Ben Roethlisberger was out with an injury, and backup quarterback Charlie Batch was taking the snaps in his absence. A backup quarterback is always an unknown element. Even a backup QB with substantial talent can be rusty from a lack of game play. In this case, 37-year-old Batch was in sync with his offense and led them to a victory on the road against a 9-2 Ravens team who were red hot on a 4-game winning streak.

The difference in this situation was likely that Batch was a 15-year veteran, who had seen more game time than most younger backups.

Joe Flacco had a poor day throwing for only 188 yards with 1 touchdown and 1 interception on 16 of 34 pass attempts. In earlier games this year, the Ravens found a way to win with low passing numbers from Flacco, but the consistent factor in those games was that Flacco did not throw an interception as he did in this game. In this contest, Flacco was sacked 3 times, which could easily have contributed to the interception.

Flacco's inconsistent quarterback stats raised the ire of some critics who thought that would certainly spell doom for the Ravens in the playoffs, especially with needing to get past New England to go to the Super Bowl. Flacco and the Ravens would prove the critics wrong through some very exciting post-season games.

With an anemic total offensive effort of 288 yards, all of Baltimore's rushers and receivers were held well under 100 yards, the highest being Ray Rice with 83 yards and a touchdown run (78 yards rushing and 5 receiving), followed by Anquan Boldin with 81 yards receiving, including a touchdown reception.

Keeping the Ravens in this game were 2 interceptions, 1 from Ed Reed and 1 from Corey Graham.

As usual, Justin Tucker was perfect with 2 of 2 field goals and 2 of 2 extra points.

This was a tough game for Ravens fans to watch as the final nail in the coffin came with literally no time to spare. Batch drove the Steelers down the field 61 yards with only a few minutes left on the clock. This set up a Shaun Suisham field goal that was kicked as time expired to win the game.

This win kept the Steelers in hopes of a playoff berth, but they would choke in their remaining games (losing 3 of 4), missing the post season altogether.

The Ravens lost this game, but still made it not only to the playoffs, but through some of the game's toughest teams all the way to the Super Bowl.

Team Leaders

Passing

Joe Flacco #5
188 Yards, 1 Touchdown, 1 Interception
(16/34, 47.06 Comp %)

Rushing

Ray Rice #27
78 Yards on 12 Carries
6.50 Yards per Carry
1 Rushing Touchdown

Bernard Pierce #30
34 Yards on 8 Carries
4.25 Yards per Carry
0 Rushing Touchdowns

Receiving

Anquan Boldin #81
81 Yards on 5 Receptions
16.20 Yards per Reception
1 Touchdown Reception

Dan Fathow 60

Vonta Leach #81
40 Yards on 4 Receptions
10.00 Yards per Reception
0 Touchdown Receptions

Torrey Smith #82
33 Yards on 3 Receptions
11.00 Yards per Reception
0 Touchdown Receptions

Dennis Pitta #88
19 Yards on 1 Reception
19.00 Yards per Reception
0 Touchdown Receptions

Kicking

Justin Tucker #9
8 Points Total
2/2 Field Goals
2/2 Extra Points

Interceptions

Corey Graham #24
1 Interception

Ed Reed #20
1 Interception

2012 – 2013 BALTIMORE RAVENS 61

THE BOTTOM LINE

9 - 3

DAN FATHOW 62

Week 14

December 9, 2012
FedEx Field – Landover, MD

Teams	1st	2nd	3rd	4th	OT	Total
Washington Redskins	14	0	6	8	3	**31**
Baltimore Ravens	7	14	0	7	**0**	**28**

GAME SUMMARY

This game was a back-and-forth fight from the beginning. The first quarter ended with the Redskins up 14-7. The second quarter ended with the Ravens up 21-14. The third quarter ended with the Ravens up 21-20. The fourth quarter ended in a tie at 28-28. The see-saw nature of this game lent itself to going into overtime.

Robert Griffin III had been the top choice for rookie of the year since his first game shocked the football world. At this point, he had led the Redskins to a 6-6 record.

In this contest, despite being sacked 3 times, Griffin had a great game throwing for 242 yards on 15 of 26 passes for 1 touchdown and 0 interceptions. On top of his passing duties, Griffin rushed for 34 yards of his own. The sad news of the day was that Griffin had been injured (sprained right knee) and taken out of the game during the Redskins final drive down the field.

Flacco had a mixed day, only throwing for 182 yards, but he did connect for 3 passing touchdowns. He was sacked twice and had 1 interception. In close games with low passing yards, whether Flacco was intercepted or not seemed to have been the deciding factor between victory and defeat.

TEAM LEADERS

Passing

Joe Flacco #5
182 Yards, 3 Touchdowns, 1 Interception
(16/21, 76.19 Comp %)

Rushing

Ray Rice #27
121 Yards on 20 Carries
6.05 Yards per Carry
1 Rushing Touchdown

Bernard Pierce #30
53 Yards on 8 Carries
6.63 Yards per Carry
0 Rushing Touchdowns

2012 – 2013 Baltimore Ravens 65

Receiving

Anquan Boldin #81
46 Yards on 5 Receptions
9.20 Yards per Reception
1 Touchdown Reception

Dennis Pitta #88
19 Yards on 1 Reception
19.00 Yards per Reception
0 Touchdown Receptions

Torrey Smith #82
21 Yards on 1 Reception
21.00 Yards per Reception
0 Touchdown Receptions

Ray Rice #27
15 Yards on 3 Receptions
5.00 Yards per Reception
0 Touchdown Receptions

Kicking

Justin Tucker #9
4 Points Total
0/0 Field Goals
4/4 Extra Points

Interceptions

None

DAN FATHOW 66

THE BOTTOM LINE
9 - 4

WEEK 15

December 16, 2012
M&T Bank Stadium – Baltimore, MD

Teams	1st	2nd	3rd	4th	Total
Denver Broncos	3	14	14	3	**34**
Baltimore Ravens	0	0	3	14	**17**

GAME SUMMARY

After losing their last 2 games, the Ravens found themselves at home facing the Denver Broncos. The Broncos were 10-3 at this point in the season, and the Ravens had a similar record of 9-4. The big difference in their records was that the Broncos were on an 8-game winning streak, not having lost since meeting New England back in Week 5. In fact, the Broncos only lost 3 games in the entire regular season, and those losses all came from playoff teams in the Atlanta Falcons, the Houston Texans, and the aforementioned New England Patriots.

In short, while both teams were talented and destined for the playoffs, the Broncos were on a big roll, and the Ravens were on a bit of a slide.

While having a low completion percentage of 50%, Joe Flacco threw for 254 yards with 1 touchdown and 1 interception. The famous opposing quarterback was none other than Payton Manning, who only threw for 204 yards with 1 touchdown and 0 interceptions.

While the Ravens beat the Broncos in the air 222 to 187 yards, they only rushed for about a third as many yards as Denver (56 to 163 rushing yards). Ray Rice was held to only 38 yards, and he accounted for all of the Ravens' rushing offense except for 20 yards put up by Bernard Pierce. Penalty yards were close with the Ravens only giving up 10 more penalty yards.

Without a lot happening on the rushing front, there were still a few highlights for the Ravens in this game. Dennis Pitta had a banner day catching 7 passes for 125 yards (an average of 17.9 yards per reception) and 2 touchdowns (which were the only 2 touchdowns for the team).

Additionally, Justin Tucker was flawless, nailing 1 of 1 field goals and 2 extra points.

The big difference in this game came from 2 factors:

1. *The Turnover War* – The Broncos were perfect in holding onto the ball in this contest, while the Ravens threw an interception and lost a fumble. 0-2 on turnovers makes it hard to win in any situation.

2. *3rd and 4th Down Efficiency* – On 3rd down efficiency, the Broncos were 5 for 16 (31%), and they did not risk going for it on 4th down at all. The Ravens were 1 for 12 (8%) on 3rd down efficiency, and they were 0 for 2 on (0%) 4th down. Denver was nearly 4 times as successful as the Ravens on 3rd down conversions, which helped them capitalize on their yardage more than their opponent.

It was a rough game for the Ravens, but they'd soon get their revenge, bumping the media-favorite Manning-led Broncos from the playoffs and putting an end to the quarterback's Cinderella, comeback season.

2012 – 2013 Baltimore Ravens

Team Leaders

Passing

Joe Flacco #5
254 Yards, 2 Touchdowns, 1 Interception
(20/40, 50 Comp %)

Rushing

Ray Rice #27
38 Yards on 12 Carries
3.17 Yards per Carry
0 Rushing Touchdowns

Bernard Pierce #30
20 Yards on 5 Carries
4.0 Yards per Carry
0 Rushing Touchdowns

Receiving

Dennis Pitta #88
125 Yards on 7 Reception
17.86 Yards per Reception
2 Touchdown Receptions

Jacoby Jones #12
51 Yards on 3 Receptions
17.00 Yards per Reception
0 Touchdown Receptions

Dan Fathow 70

Tandon Doss #17
28 Yards on 2 Reception
14.00 Yards per Reception
0 Touchdown Receptions

David Reed #16
22 Yards on 2 Receptions
11.00 Yards per Reception
0 Touchdown Receptions

Kicking

Justin Tucker #9
5 Points Total
1/1 Field Goals
2/2 Extra Points

Interceptions

none

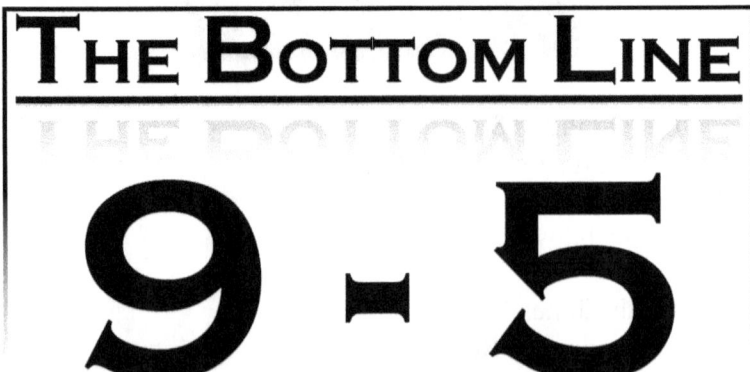

The Bottom Line

9 - 5

WEEK 16

December 23, 2012
M&T Bank Stadium – Baltimore, MD

Teams	1st	2nd	3rd	4th	Total
New York Giants	7	0	0	7	**14**
Baltimore Ravens	14	10	3	6	**33**

GAME SUMMARY

Let's take a few steps back in time before we look at Week 16. Going into Week 13, the Baltimore Ravens were not only 9-2, not only were they considered a serious post season threat, but they were Super Bowl contenders.

Jump forward 3 weeks, and the Ravens were on a 3-game losing streak, dropping down to a 9-5 record. The Ravens went from being considered as one of the top teams in all football to a team that had lost its momentum. Bandwagon critics were plentiful, being very quick to dismiss the Ravens, who had done so much earlier in the season, as a team that didn't have that championship killer instinct.

Their opponents were the 8-6 New York Giants.

If the Ravens won this game, they'd become the 2012 AFC North Champions, a distinction that they've been waiting to earn with a single victory over the previous 3 winless weeks. Almost more important than that, the Ravens needed a win to both boost their own confidence level and silence the critical media.

On the other hand, if the Giants lost this game, they would be ceiling the coffin on their playoff hopes. Both teams had a lot to play for. Facing Eli Manning in a game that had the Giants playoff hopes on the line was to be no easy task based on past history.

Not only did Baltimore win, but they won by 19 points, which was more than double the points that they allowed the Giants to score. This decisive victory over the 8-6 Giants was more than enough to stick it to the haters and to end their 3 game skid, redirecting their course back to the post season and their pursuit of the Super Bowl.

So, how did it all go down?

First of all, the Baltimore defense shut Eli Manning down, holding him to a measly 150 yards with a 50% completion ratio and 1 touchdown. Manning was sacked 3 times during this game, while Joe Flacco was not sacked at all.

Speaking of Flacco, he was the other key ingredient in this decisive win. Flacco threw for 309 yards on 25 of 36 passes for 2 touchdowns and 0 interceptions. If that weren't enough, Flacco rushed into the end zone himself for a touchdown.

The Ravens offense was killing on both sides of the ball with 2 players rushing for over 100 yards (Pierce and Rice) and 2 players receiving for about 90 yards (Boldin and Smith). All told, the Ravens put up a total of 533 yards, crushing the Giants total of 186 yards.

The kicking game was also firing with Justin Tucker putting 15 points on the board from 3 of 3 field goals and 4 of 4 extra points.

The only area of the game where the Giants were in the same ballpark as the Ravens was turnovers, in which neither team had one. Part of that might be related to the Giants only having the ball for 20:39, while the Ravens had the ball for nearly twice as long at 39:21.

In summary, the Ravens had double the time of possession, nearly 3 times the total yardage, a conversion rate of 61% on 3rd down, and 0 turnovers. That is a recipe for total domination, and that was exactly what happened to the Giants when they came to Baltimore.

The Ravens won the AFC North Championship in style and were on their way to the big game.

Team Leaders

Passing

Joe Flacco #5
309 Yards, 2 Touchdowns, 0 Interceptions
(25/36, 69.44 Comp %)

Rushing

Bernard Pierce #30
123 Yards on 14 Carries
8.79 Yards per Carry
0 Rushing Touchdowns

Ray Rice #27
107 Yards on 24 Carries
4.50 Yards per Carry
0 Rushing Touchdowns

Joe Flacco #5
-10 Yards on 3 Carries
-3.33 Yards per Carry
1 Rushing Touchdown

Dan Fathow 74

Receiving

Anquan Boldin #81
93 Yards on 7 Receptions
13.29 Yards per Reception
0 Touchdown Receptions

Torrey Smith #82
88 Yards on 5 Reception
17.60 Yards per Reception
1 Touchdown Reception

Dennis Pitta #88
56 Yards on 4 Reception
14.00 Yards per Reception
0 Touchdown Receptions

Ray Rice #27
51 Yards on 6 Receptions
8.50 Yards per Reception
1 Touchdown Reception

Kicking

Justin Tucker #9
15 Points Total
4/4 Field Goals
3/3 Extra Points

2012 – 2013 Baltimore Ravens 75

Interceptions

none

The Bottom Line

10 - 5

DAN FATHOW 76

Week 17

December 30, 2012
Paul Brown Stadium – Cincinnati, OH

Teams	1st	2nd	3rd	4th	Total
Cincinnati Bengals	0	7	6	10	**23**
Baltimore Ravens	7	0	0	10	**17**

GAME SUMMARY

Having already won the AFC North Championship and having secured their spot in the playoffs, the Ravens really had nothing to play for in this game. The Bengals were 9-6, very close to the Ravens' record of 10-5, and their playoff spot was also already clinched. With nothing to gain and everything to lose in the form of injuries, many starters were benched on both teams to keep them healthy for the playoffs.

Snaps in this game were taken mostly by backup quarterback Tyrod Taylor, who went 15 for 25 for 149 yards, 0 touchdowns, and 1 interception. Taylor was sacked 3 times, but he also ran in a touchdown.

Despite putting up 352 total yards, which was 163 yards above their opponent, the Ravens lost this game, partially due to losing the turnover battle 0-1 and partially due to 10 penalties accounting for 102 yards. With a total of 542 yards of offense from both teams, this certainly was a lame-duck rivalry game with nothing riding on its outcome.

The Bengals may have won this game, but they'd be out of the playoffs in the first round, courtesy of the Houston Texans, who would go on to lose to the New England Patriots, who would in turn go on to lose to the Baltimore Ravens.

Team Leaders

Passing

Tyrod Taylor #2
149 Yards, 0 Touchdowns, 1 Interception
(15/25, 60.00 Comp %)

Rushing

Bernard Pierce #30
89 Yards on 22 Carries
4.05 Yards per Carry
0 Rushing Touchdowns

Tyrod Taylor #2
65 Yards on 9 Carries
7.20 Yards per Carry
0 Rushing Touchdowns

Anthony Allen #35
41 Yards on 10 Carries
4.10 Yards per Carry
1 Rushing Touchdown

Receiving

Ed Dickson #84
64 Yards on 6 Receptions
10.67 Yards per Reception
0 Touchdown Receptions

David Reed #16
44 Yards on 3 Reception
14.67 Yards per Reception
0 Touchdown Receptions

Jacoby Jones #12
36 Yards on 3 Reception
12.00 Yards per Reception
0 Touchdown Receptions

Deonte Thompson #83
26 Yards on 4 Receptions
6.50 Yards per Reception
0 Touchdown Receptions

Kicking

Justin Tucker #9
5 Points Total
1/2 Field Goals
2/2 Extra Points

Interceptions

none

DAN FATHOW 80

THE BOTTOM LINE

10 - 6

WEEK 18

January 6, 2013
M&T Bank Stadium – Baltimore, MD

Teams	1st	2nd	3rd	4th	Total
Indianapolis Colts	0	6	3	0	9
Baltimore Ravens	0	10	7	7	24

GAME SUMMARY

The Ravens started off the playoffs and the new year at home in the AFC Wild Card Game which was played on January 6, 2013.

Baltimore was facing the Indianapolis Colts, who were 11-5 in the regular season, and many pundits' choice for a Super Bowl contender. Once RG3 was injured, Colts' quarterback Andrew Luck became one of the front-runners for rookie of the year, being lauded for his ability to stay calm under pressure and deliver key plays when they were needed.

Many of the pre-game sports analysts talked about the advantage going to the Colts, because Luck was a more consistent quarterback, especially under pressure. The game itself proved this common analysis to be wrong.

While Luck had a good game throwing for 288 yards, he had 0 touchdowns and 1 interception. The Ravens' defense did get to him, sacking him 3 times during the game. Joe Flacco threw for nearly the same amount of yards at 282 with 2 touchdowns and 0 interceptions. Flacco was only sacked once, and he played a calm, consistent game, contradicting overly-negative critics and helping his team move on in the playoffs. Flacco also set a record for being the only quarterback to win at least 1 post-season game in all 5 of his professional seasons.

Setting a Ravens' team record, Anquan Boldin caught for 145 yards. He did so on 5 receptions, with an average of 29 yards on each one, and that included a touchdown grab.

One of the only negatives of the game for Baltimore came in the form of Ray Rice's uncharacteristic 2 fumbles that were picked up by Indianapolis, his only 2 fumbles of the entire season. However, turnovers were tied at 2 apiece, with an interception and a fumble from the Colts.

Another of the areas where the Ravens dominated was in red zone offense. The Colts were 0 for 3 in the red zone, while the Ravens were 3 for 5. Indianapolis were also 0 for 2 on 4th down, while the Ravens did not go for it on 4th down.

This game was also bitter-sweet for longtime Ravens fans as it marked Ray Lewis's last game in M&T Bank Stadium in Baltimore.

The 24-9 trouncing of the favored Colts was a wake-up call for the doubting media and all other playoff teams that the Ravens would be a dangerous opponent to contend with.

Team Leaders

Passing

Joe Flacco #5
282 Yards, 2 Touchdowns, 0 Interceptions
(12/23, 52.17 Comp %)

2012 – 2013 Baltimore Ravens

Rushing

Bernard Pierce #30
103 Yards on 13 Carries
7.92 Yards per Carry
0 Rushing Touchdowns

Ray Rice #27
68 Yards on 15 Carries
4.53 Yards per Carry
0 Rushing Touchdowns

Vonta Leach #44
2 Yards on 1 Carry
2.00 Yards per Carry
1 Rushing Touchdown

Receiving

Anquan Boldin #81
145 Yards on 5 Receptions
29 Yards per Reception
1 Touchdown Reception

Ray Rice #27
47 Yards on 1 Reception
47 Yards per Reception
0 Touchdown Receptions

Torrey Smith #82
31 Yards on 2 Receptions
15.50 Yards per Reception
1 Touchdown Reception

Dennis Pitta #88
27 Yards on 2 Receptions
13.50 Yards per Reception
1 Touchdown Reception

Ed Dickson #84
24 Yards on 1 Reception
24.00 Yards per Reception
0 Touchdown Receptions

Kicking

Justin Tucker #9
6 Points Total
1/1 Field Goals
3/3 Extra Points

Interceptions

none

The Bottom Line

11 - 6

Week 19

January 12, 2013
Sports Authority Field – Denver, CO

Teams	1st	2nd	3rd	4th	OT1	OT2	Total
Denver Broncos	14	7	7	7	0	0	35
Baltimore Ravens	14	7	7	7	0	3	38

GAME SUMMARY

The Ravens said they wanted to meet the Denver Broncos in the AFC Divisional Playoff. After their embarrassing 34-17 loss to the Broncos in Week 15, Baltimore wanted a chance to vindicate themselves.

Coming into this game, the Broncos were on an 11-game winning streak, 13-4 overall, and they were heavy favorites to not only win this game, but the Super Bowl itself. In fact, the common prediction was that the Broncos would beat the Ravens by at least 9.5 points. Pay attention to that 9.5-point prediction; it will come up again in about a week.
(http://espn.go.com/blog/afcnorth/post/_/id/64042/wake-up-call-super-ravens)

At first look, the above scoreboard would seem to be a mistake with both teams having the same exact score and total through the first 4 quarters and 1st overtime. The numbers are correct because this game was an evenly-matched, back-and-forth battle from start to finish.

Ray Rice had a great rushing game, racking up 131 yards on 30 carries, including a 1 touchdown.

On the receiving front, Torrey Smith caught 3 receptions for 98 yards and 2 touchdowns. In addition to Smith, Jones and Boldin both caught for over 70 yards with Jones also getting a touchdown grab.

In this contest, Joe Flacco outperformed Peyton Manning. Flacco put up 331 yards and 3 touchdowns with 0 interceptions, while Manning put up 290 yards and 3 touchdowns with 2 interceptions. Manning did have a better completion percentage at 65.11, compared to Flacco's 52.94; however, Manning's 2 interceptions went a long way to wiping out whatever advantage the completion percentage might have offered.

Justin Tucker was the big hero of the day as he sealed the win for the Ravens by kicking a 47–yard field goal in double overtime, sending the Broncos home for an early spring training and his own team marching on to face the New England Patriots in the AFC Championship Game.

Team Leaders

Passing

Joe Flacco #5
331 Yards, 3 Touchdowns, 0 Interceptions
(18/34, 52.94 Comp %)

Rushing

Ray Rice #27
131 Yards on 30 Carries
4.37 Yards per Carry
1 Rushing Touchdown

2012 – 2013 Baltimore Ravens 87

Bernard Pierce #30
14 Yards on 5 Carries
2.80 Yards per Carry
0 Rushing Touchdowns

Vonta Leach #44
3 Yards on 1 Carry
3.00 Yards per Carry
0 Rushing Touchdowns

Receiving

Torrey Smith #82
98 Yards on 3 Receptions
32.67 Yards per Reception
2 Touchdown Receptions

Jacoby Jones #12
77 Yards on 2 Receptions
36.5 Yards per Reception
1 Touchdown Reception

Anquan Boldin #81
71 Yards on 6 Receptions
11.83 Yards per Reception
0 Touchdown Receptions

Dennis Pitta #88
55 Yards on 3 Receptions
18.33 Yards per Reception
1 Touchdown Reception

Ed Dickson #84
29 Yards on 3 Reception
9.67 Yards per Reception
0 Touchdown Receptions

Dan Fathow 88

Kicking

Justin Tucker #9
8 Points Total
1/1 Field Goals
5/5 Extra Points

Interceptions

Corey Graham #24
1 Interception Run Back for a Touchdown

The Bottom Line
12 - 6

WEEK 20

January 20, 2013
Gillette Stadium – Foxboro, MA

Teams	1st	2nd	3rd	4th	Total
New England Patriots	3	10	0	0	13
Baltimore Ravens	0	7	7	14	28

GAME SUMMARY

The Ravens shocked most of the sports world in the previous week with their nail-biting, edge-of-your-seat, Hollywood-movie victory over the Denver Broncos, who were rampaging their way through their opponents for the last 11 games.

The Ravens stopped the unstoppable juggernaut on the road in adverse conditions in Mile High, Denver, Colorado. You'd think that would earn the respect of the sports media. You'd be wrong.

For the second week in a row, the Ravens were picked to lose to a team led by a high-profile quarterback by 9.5 points. For the second week in a row, Joe Flacco was said to be incapable of keeping up with the likes of a top-tier quarterback: Payton Manning in the previous week and Tom Brady this week. For the second week in a row, the sports experts were proven wrong and had grossly underestimated both Joe Flacco and the Baltimore Ravens.

At halftime, things were not looking great for the Ravens. The scoreboard read 13-7 in favor of the Patriots. However, the second half was all Baltimore Ravens. In the 3rd quarter, the Ravens defense shut down Tom Brady and the Pats, keeping them scoreless, while they scored a touchdown of their own, taking a 1-point lead. The Ravens would not lose this lead, stretching it to a healthy 15-points by the game's end with 2 more touchdowns in the 4th quarter.

Certainly no one would have predicted that the Patriots, who were the 4th-best passing team and the 7th-best rushing team in all of the NFL, to be completely shut out in the entire second half. That was an undeniable sign that the Baltimore Ravens were a championship caliber team who were capable of beating any opponent, even on the road, with all the pressure of the entire sports world watching.

The crux of this competition really came down to turnovers. The Ravens defense forced 3 turnovers, and the Ravens offense did not surrender the ball at all. A 0-3 turnover deficit is hard to overcome in the NFL, and the Patriots were certainly not able to even make this a close game. Once the Ravens pulled ahead, the Patriots never got back on the scoreboard.

A 15-point victory over the heavily-favored Patriots was the exact kind of vindication that the Ravens needed and their fans were clamoring for.

How did the quarterbacks match up?

Here are the numbers: Tom Brady had a powerful passing performance with 320 yards, but he only connected for 1 touchdown with 2 costly interceptions. Joe Flacco had less yardage at 240 yards, but he had an impressive 3 touchdowns with 0 interceptions. Despite being sacked twice, Flacco proved to have the more reliable hand in the game, never giving up the ball and successfully throwing into the end zone 3 times.

In the air, the Ravens had 3 receivers catching for over 50 yards. Torrey Smith had 69 yards on 4 catches. Anquan Boldin nabbed 2 touchdowns and 60 yards on 5 passes. And,

Dennis Pitta also grabbed 1 touchdown and 55 yards on 5 receptions.

On the rushing front, Bernard Pierce and Ray Rice both ran for about 50 yards each, Rice also rushing into the end zone.

Ray Lewis led the defense with a great game, making 14 tackles, 6 of them as solo tackles. Corey Graham was next up on defense with 11 tackles, 4 of them being solo tackles.

Team Leaders

Passing

Joe Flacco #5
240 Yards, 3 Touchdowns, 0 Interceptions
(21/36, 58.33 Comp %)

Rushing

Bernard Pierce #30
52 Yards on 9 Carries
5.78 Yards per Carry
0 Rushing Touchdowns

Ray Rice #27
48 Yards on 19 Carries
2.53 Yards per Carry
1 Rushing Touchdown

Dan Fathow 92

Receiving

Torrey Smith #82
69 Yards on 4 Receptions
17.25 Yards per Reception
0 Touchdown Receptions

Anquan Boldin #81
60 Yards on 5 Receptions
12.00 Yards per Reception
2 Touchdown Receptions

Dennis Pitta #88
55 Yards on 5 Receptions
11.00 Yards per Reception
1 Touchdown Reception

Ray Rice #27
22 Yards on 3 Receptions
7.33 Yards per Reception
0 Touchdown Receptions

Vonta Leach #44
20 Yards on 2 Receptions
10.00 Yards per Reception
0 Touchdown Receptions

Kicking

Justin Tucker #9
4 Points Total
0/0 Field Goals
4/4 Extra Points

2012 – 2013 Baltimore Ravens 93

Interceptions

Dannell Ellerbe #59
1 Interception

Cary Williams #29
1 Interception

The Bottom Line

13 - 6

AFC Champions

DAN FATHOW 94

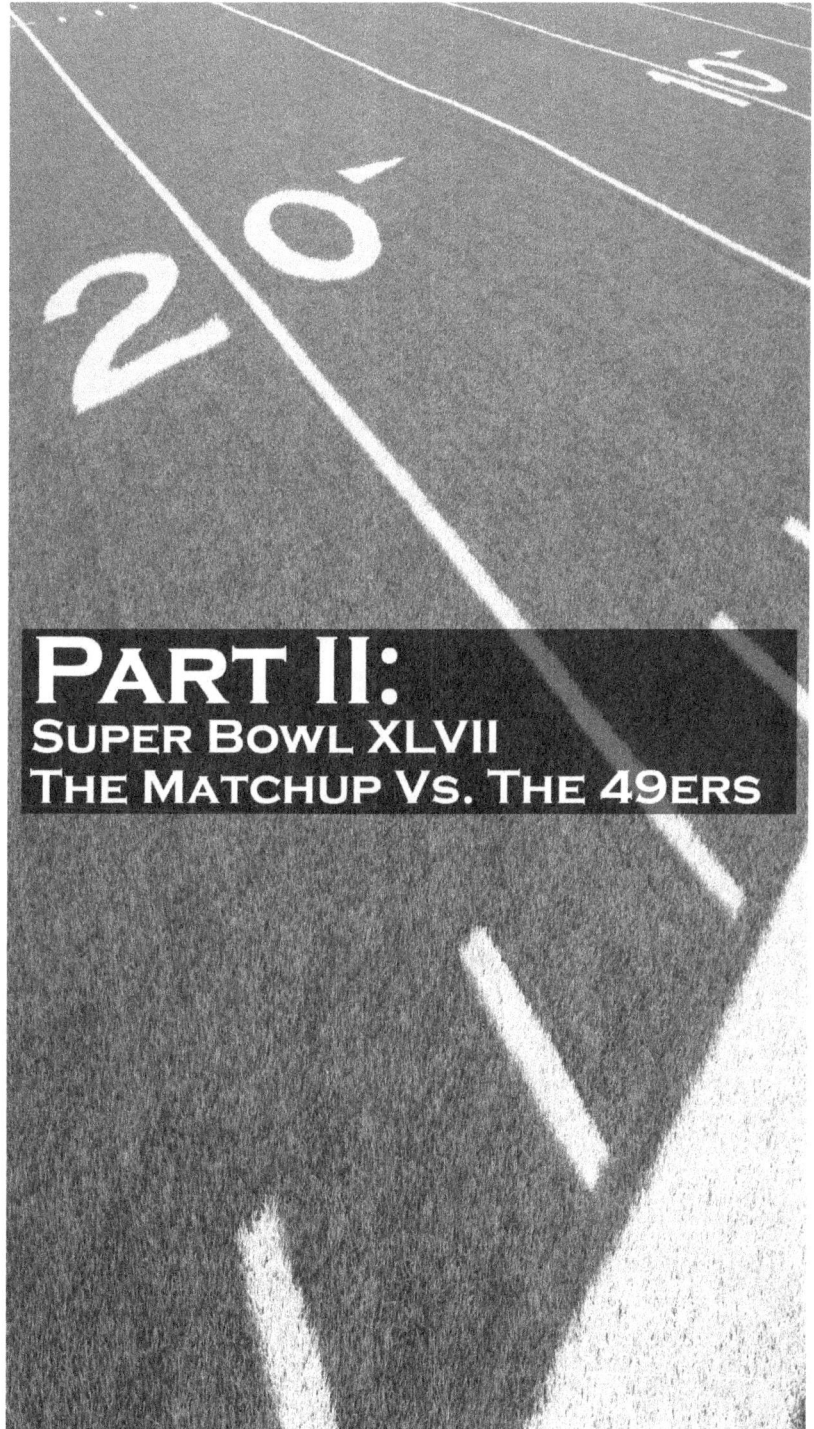

PART II:
SUPER BOWL XLVII
THE MATCHUP VS. THE 49ERS

DAN FATHOW 96

The Super Bowl XLVII Matchup

In the regular season, the Baltimore Ravens were 10-6, and the San Francisco 49ers were 11-4-1. Here are some key stats on how they both battled their way to the big game, side-by-side for a direct comparison.

TEAM	Points Scored	Points Allowed
Ravens	398	344
49ers	397	273

Team Passing Statistics

TEAM	Comp	Attempts	Comp %	Yards	TDs	Interceptions
Ravens	334	560	59.64%	3739	22	11
49ers	289	436	66.28%	3298	23	8

At first glance it would appear that the Ravens with 11 interceptions are throwing more passes away than the 49ers; however, there is more to it than that. The Ravens had 124 more pass attempts and 45 more completions than the 49ers. For every 54.5 pass attempts, the 49ers had 1 interception. For every 50.9 pass attempts, the Ravens threw 1 interception. There is not likely to be 50 pass attempts by either team, so it's hard to say who will throw more interceptions. The pressure of playing in the big game is likely to be a bigger factor in throwing an interception than regular season statistics. The other variable that is throwing some of the figures off is that nearly 8 games of the 49ers statistics were based on Alex Smith's performance and not Colin Kaepernick's.

In passing yards, the Ravens have the upper hand with having thrown 441 more yards than the 49ers. However, if you divide that by 16 games, the difference is 27.56 more passing yards per game, which is not that much of a difference or an advantage.

The 49ers have a higher completion ratio, but once again, that stat is colored with Alex Smith's figures. Kaepernick's regular season completion percentage is a bit lower at 62.4%, but that is still 2.76% higher than the Ravens' average. All in all, the passing numbers are fairly close for both teams.

Team Rushing Statistics

TEAM	Carries	Yards	Average	Touchdowns
Ravens	444	1901	4.28 Yards	17
49ers	492	2491	5.06 Yards	17

The rushing numbers are also not too far apart. The 49ers rushed for more yards, with a higher average of 5.06 yards per carry, which is 0.78 yards more per carry than the Ravens. While 0.78 of a yard more per carry may not seem like much, it is 28.08 inches more or 2 feet 4 inches more per carry than the Ravens. When first downs and even touchdowns often come down to inches, this may or may not be a factor in this contest.

Both teams rushed for 17 touchdowns, so they have about equal ability to run the ball in to the end zone.

Team Kicking Statistics

TEAM	Extra Points	Extra Point %	Field Goals Made	Field Goals Attempted	Field Goal %	Total Points
Ravens	42	100%	30	33	90.90%	132
49ers	44	100%	29	42	69.04%	131

A cursory glance at points made might lead one to believe the kicking game is about even, but the Baltimore Ravens have a decisive advantage in the kicking game. The key is the field goal percentage. While the Ravens hit 30 field goals for 90 points and the 49ers hit 29 field goals for 87 points, Baltimore did it on 33 attempts, while it took the 49ers 42 attempts. So, that's 9 more attempts to kick 1 less field goal. Statistically, the Ravens are hitting 91% of their field goals, while the 49ers are only hitting 69% of their field goals. That is a significant difference that could easily effect the outcome of this game.

TEAM DEFENSIVE TURNOVERS

TEAM	Interceptions	Fumbles
Ravens	13	12
49ers	14	11

The defensive turnovers are very close. The Ravens have one more interception, while the 49ers have one more fumble resulting in a turnover. The ability of each team to force turnovers is nearly identical.

Quarterback Matchup
Flacco vs. Kaepernick

By the numbers:

Joe Flacco
Career Stats

Year	CMP	ATT	YDS	CMP%	TD	INT
2012	317	531	3,817	59.70	22	10
2011	312	542	3,610	57.56	20	12
2010	306	489	3,622	62.58	25	10
2009	315	499	3,613	63.13	21	12
2008	257	428	2,971	60.05	14	12

2012 Stats Chart
Regular Season - Post – Career

	CMP	ATT	YDS	CMP%	Avg	TD	INT
2012 Regular Season	317	531	3,817	59.70	7.19	22	10

2012 Postseason	51	93	853	54.84	9.17	8	0
Career	1,507	2,489	17,633	60.54	7.08	102	56

COLIN KAEPERNICK
CAREER STATS

Year	CMP	ATT	YDS	CMP%	TD	INT
2012	136	218	1,814	62.39	10	3
2011	3	5	35	60.00	0	0

2012 STATS CHART
REGULAR SEASON - POST – CAREER

	CMP	ATT	YDS	CMP%	AVG	TD	INT
2012 Regular Season	136	218	1,814	62.39	8.32	10	3
2012 Postseason	33	52	496	63.46	9.54	3	1
Career	139	223	1,849	62.33	8.29	10	3

The experience factor hands down goes to Joe Flacco, who has been in the league for 5 years, holding a record for winning at least 1 playoff game in all 5 years of his pro career.

While many have focused on Kaepernick's explosive, record-setting running performance in the post season, Flacco has better numbers as a passing quarterback. Flacco has passed for 8 touchdowns with 0 interceptions in the post season, while Kaepernick has only passed for 3 touchdowns with 1 interception. Flacco also threw for nearly double the yards as Kaepernick, 853-496 (1.72 times as many yards as his opponent). However, Kaepernick has a better completion percentage, albeit on fewer passes, of 63.46% to Flacco's 54.84%.

Without Kaepernick's running game, Flacco would clearly be the most effective quarterback in the 2013 post season. But if Kaepernick rushes anywhere in the ballpark of the amazing 181 yards that he put up against Green Bay, it will be very hard for the Ravens to compete, barring a lot of failed 3rd and 4th down conversions and/or turnovers. The obvious other side of the coin is that if the Ravens shut down Kaepernick's rushing game, Flacco should be able to lead his team to victory. That's where the Kaepernick-Smith quarterback controversy could really become an advantage for the Ravens.

Check out more great releases from
Megalodon Entertainment LLC

Follow the New Orleans Saints through their amazing **Super Bowl XLIV (44) Championship** season, and re-experience every game, relive every score, and savor every victory. Travel with The Saints on their long, often trying 43 years on the road to success. Compare the stats on every Saints Quarterback. Who has the most yards, wins, and completions? Archie Manning, Drew Brees, Bobby Hebert, or Aaron Brooks? Find out which Saints coach has the best record and the most games. Sean Payton, Jim Mora, or Bum Phillips? This book is the perfect companion for new and long-time Saints fans alike.

ISBN 978-0-9800605-7-7

ALSO BY DAN FATHOW
THE 2012-2013 ALABAMA CRIMSON TIDE

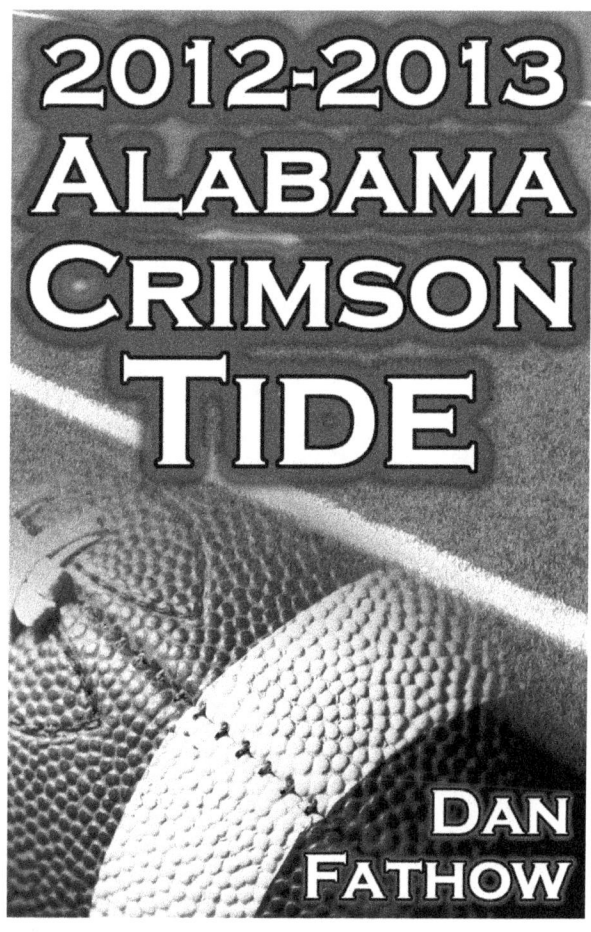

The defending BCS national champions, the 2012 Alabama Crimson Tide, dominated opponents throughout the season, earning a repeat trip to the 2013 BCS National Championship Game. Quarterback A.J. McCarron had a stellar year, putting up great numbers and leading his team back to the big game. Legendary coach Nick Saban kept his team focused and playing sharp, smart football all year long, becoming SEC Champions along the way. Follow the Crimson Tide as they destroy opponents, including their rival LSU Tigers and the Georgia Bulldogs in two of the most exciting and most talked about games of the year. Relive the magical 2012 season, victory by victory, quarter by quarter, and score by score all the way to the 2013 BCS National Championship Game against the Notre Dame Fighting Irish.

ISBN: 978-1-61589-038-5

www.ingramcontent.com/pod-product-compliance
Lightning Source LLC
Chambersburg PA
CBHW070513090426
42735CB00012B/2769